S0-AIY-761

biography of water

biography of water

carrie bennett

winner of the 2004

washington prize

THE WORD WORKS

WASHINGTON, D.C.

The WORD WORKS
PO Box 42164
Washington, DC 20015
editor@wordworksdc.com

Cover art: Grid 017a (front) and Grid 017b (back)
            by Kelvy Bird

Book design, typography by Janice Olson

Library of Congress Number: 2004114203
International Standard Book Number: 0-915380-58-7

acknowledgments

grateful acknowledgement to the editors of the following journals
in which these selections first appeared:

So to Speak:
from "toward spring," never easy to say this

88:
from "covered the mark," of course you anticipated this
from "a fundamental history," the hand no longer rests

Phoebe:
from "a fundamental history," listen there is a background

for my parents

contents

introduction　8

covered the mark　**11**

biography of water　**17**

a scene at dawn　**23**

a fundamental history　**29**

what the body offers the room (1)　**41**

what the body offers the room (2)　**49**

toward season　**57**

about the Washington Prize　68
about the author　69
about the Word Works　70
Word Works books　71

introduction

What does it mean for the constructed we to dissolve?

What is the path of such a transformation?

How do we inhabit loss?

Bennett's book length poem *biography of water* chronicles a body's return to its gaze in the world. Here biography is not a linear account of events and experiences but rather a reflection of the gaze of a self in dissolution. "The appearance of the gaze belongs to the disappearance of the self," Eli Friedlander argues. Images of the inhabited landscape enter the physical space of the body. The boundaries between the self and the world dissolve. The visual field, the places where the gaze dwells, is suddenly without distinction from the she who regards. Then the illusion of unity is unsettling and out of the natural order: "she is landscape and/ flat board blue against steel/ you blue you in mouth you/ fell you/ want to remember you/ yes."

Dwelling places (where the gaze dwells) quickly displace the subject in this poem. These background spaces become the active forces— landscape, oceans, sky, rooms, their windows, houses, yards, and cities lose their outer world distinction. The entrance of these external spaces through the gaze allows them to fill all the physiological space abdicated by the she. It is, for example, as if the water that constitutes seventy percent of the human body rejoined the water that covers seventy percent of the earth: "she let the body do what it had to and what it did meant water in the throat." The dissolve into an external identity creates a morbid tension within the poem. "Is this what it means to end," the poet asks.

The generic descriptions (land, sky, bird) and pronominal use that dominate this long poem, of seven sections, contribute to its atmosphere of loss and damage. This rhetorical strategy releases the poem from biographical time and lands it in a seasonal cycle. Brilliantly it is the subject's ability to recognize seasonal change as spring approaches that allows the external world to be external again.

Biography of water is that rare achievement where simplicity and transparency is maneuvered into its most complex stance. The language here is never unfamiliar or strained and yet some of the most complicated exploration of the loss of self occurs in this extended poem.

Claudia Rankine,

author of *Don't Let Me Be Lonely*

She gazed back over the sea, at the island. But the leaf was losing its sharpness. It was very small; it was very distant. The sea was more important now than the shore. Waves were all round them, tossing and sinking, with a log wallowing down one wave; a gull riding another. About here, she thought, dabbling her fingers in the water, a ship had sunk, and she murmured, dreamily half asleep, how we perished, each alone.

—Virginia Woolf, *To the Lighthouse*

covered the mark

you roll over and break (thus is the thinness of bone)

                             here is where night begins :
slow tendering
        of a faded sky   watch the curling of melon-
                                   colored tulips
have you learned yet to count

the days are gone
the days are not gone   indistinguishable

(now there is enough skin to piece together as proof)

you are rehabilitated : a shadow across a gray sky

you are the one nobody waits for
            the one for whom there are
                no arrivals last minute in the last hours   of night

thin is the stem that bends in no breeze   you wouldn't make it
            in this weather   with waves up to here and
a water always wanting more
                    of your body than   you want to give

of course you anticipated this
the light falling through the screen that way

how does something look
                          like gold
in the back of a throat a house of numbered rooms

we were the couple
swimming in the gulf
                          the only two
the sky the water
the pine trees twisting
the sand
                          when all the days
started leading away
                          then

everywhere spindled points burst
from branches leaves bud
                            immediately fall
what is left fits

when the end arrives the body knows this time this door this
                                              clicked nail

you uncover the skin the bone
why isn't night yet
                    almost resisting

biography of water

                                        she is landscape and

                    flat board blue against steel
you blue you in mouth you
fell you   want to remember you   yes

counting weeks
                        across the trees this turning snow away

one hand makes the underneath of sand
                                        the bottom drifted

to the trees lining miles :
                                that is lake
                                this is sky
a floor of sand and
                    leaf you left the windows open this time

against sky water against a noise like prayer a hymnal already
against the oddness   the captured moment
                      and the disappearance
of a filled hand :
                    (lake loon birch tree

two figures make
         a record   among the fallen leaves are
everywhere

                some bird bleeds
from beak and eyes
a piece of light shadowed into

                how many shades of green :
how many walls to cover

tomorrow already was
a repeated noise in the background

I wanted this
last minute ringing
                when two bodies touch
they are still two bodies

and what is left
to ask is asked
                too late the air attaches
there are unnamed flowers

                        in this ravine of wooden doorways
                                evening has arrived
: light that falls
when we are unable to catch
                        the instant unmoving

how does a body move through rooms knowing what is next :
this is not the next step
to a reconciliation
        doesn't matter the leaf awkwardly twisted outline and
what becomes of us
when we are no longer in viewing distance

we evaporate under a thumb
your left hand divisible by my left
                              a sectioned body
faltering against
              another sectioned body

strung to green-leafed and light it doesn't stop ringing
this talk itself
                  tongues litter the ground litter
the body
that walks on them

                    there is nothing to offer you
water is gliding across water

holding itself up
                    with a piece of wind

scene at dawn

✣

they are not the dark leaves
were never the dark leaves never

anything but
       patterned departures an insistence for

           the precise
         instant of release to say :

o hidden garment o twisted piece
of iron : this is my body

so disjointed only an opened
neck reduced
           to the thinness of cracks
I am the object that waits
in the pre-light sky and

these are the colors : yellow brown

✣

in this tomorrow
          one bird sounding
one note

✤

kept to yourself a network of wires buzz :
this is the heart at work : blood

    rushing through
         abbreviated limbs

of organs : they work themselves
into the sky
      contains the same
material pushed aside

✤

        the body acts as container
the continued flight unfolded

this weight of position the hand reaching
to find itself
out of habit

✣

it happens that
                the morning is thrown back over

the swept up sky
the sounds muted against the sheeted air

drawn into one the notes layer
their origin unseen
                but enough to know

                somewhere a settled bird
makes that sound

✣

the view's movements hardly there
only a continuous tremble
                of green on branch

the shape of leaf distant
indistinct
                until the sky is a pause

behind a very small scene

✧

left to itself the ground follows orders
whatever season it is

✧

I know that glass stops movement but

still too early
        from this view
                                    there is no
movement
        only planes of mostly blue

                        down below the houses are paper thin

the early shadow on the ground the
starting sounds of day : rain against
cement and dirt

that shadow creates pockets of light : a lamp lit
through pulled blinds the stillness

the winding up and mostly
                        the solitary perspective
                    of each detail
stretching into shape

✧

though my tongue is thin and
                    the sounds sometimes
                    don't make sense
in themselves

a fundamental history

the hand no longer rests
what flies flies away and

there are two
of everything

where do the lined figures go
the bird's wings fall off

a formal breath
in the wrong element

the depths of which are gone
immobile

are stationary horizons
this is the sum of a bent figure

a hole in the ground fills
sand and water under each :

it opened the night
opened the eye stitched shut

the days eventually end
the day with too much

listen : there is a background backed into a wall
nothing bright a blooming about

this skinned petal
the key is lost and locked out

a brief passing
of opened windows

maybe nothing is transmitted though the wires
it is the sand creeping back into the ocean

the road covered with gulls
on either side there is water

it drifts away
it pulls you in

we made a birdhouse of what was lost
here is the wall

which breathes here
we stepped over

our bodies
in hallways grown over each leaf and

so strange dwelling you opened me
I left what openings I could

we admit we close our eyes
just long enough

all the forwarding addresses billed
the evidence pushed out the windows

whom do we propose to now
that the shades are drawn

to the mistaken songbird go home
the hour's business is done

this isn't the sun but
the ground given up

our tongues sold for a drafty stone
your hand a bridged water

up here what color would you call this
view of lowering

windows caught
my throat through

sky shattered
by branches

in this hour we place our palms to glass
see what holds when nothing moves

an object left to itself
we only have two eyes to close we should be so lucky

no wings left to rest the scattering
what is while in this ground

we are fitted we
touch this and it takes root

now is not the time
to open our pockets

snow falls in a corner
and nothing holds

unless the view is a backdrop
it doesn't matter how much the snow costs

considering
our bodies around each block we say

this is the inside of my hand
we point to a bird

outside pecking
the ground through

what we mean is : it isn't easy
this note held longer

than the breath
and you smallest one

deliver the first unfolding
as if your figure goes here

unformed or not disregard
these colors

won't last much longer
once you've opened the door

one leaf doesn't tell us much
though

we memorize the placement
of things :

this hemmed print here this
pocketed eye there we say

open the open and
step carefully for isn't a sidewalk there to leave on

what the body offers the room
(1)

find this city

under a streetlight
brickwall and windowpane and   (the pause
                                      before entering a street
                                      to open a door to know
                                      what you're getting into
                                      before you get in)

o building o unexpected moment
standing at the corner with hand raised

here : a circled piece of cement illuminated
here : materials are drawn into the mouth
are unknown though settling
at the back of the throat   when the scene opens it is night

where do eyes go when shut when is the proper time to leave
                                      escorted by a blinking light

there's nothing between you and the tiled floor

and everything is sold:
(the trip to some city two years ago
on the train the railing streaked and greasy)

see the branches are missing
lifted
into graphed meeting places :

a building in my right eye

a building
in my left

this is only nightfall

this is a tremble in the sky

a background noise gone noticed

in the scene :   slanted doorstep
                        a plant with bright blooms
                        bricks straight up a building side
                        glass squared off the sun
                        glass cutting a home in the wall
                        glass reflecting
                        the movement of temperature
                        means to get from block to block
                        paint unpeeling to rain
                        dirt in piles
                        small fences around trees

the backdrop darkens

to the color of branches   the space between closes its eyes

salvage the red

tomorrow was never new

in that picture such a close-up don't you ever wish

your hand on the railing you watch the city beneath

again a slanted doorway
                              in the aired fallings
          a leaf returned

what eye yields a figure
again and what houred moment lasts

to make it skin thrown over
                    these bones broken from their outline

now we board the vents now we
nail the windows shut
                to prevent the air from leaving we climb
                under the covers we pull the shades
                we wait

you manage to eat the dark

the falling is in your pocket

the view caught leaning

we pretend the sky is an opened mouth

begins : or : to say

               our need for origin

persists though we believe

in exact measures :

               how when a door is closed it stays
               that way

we pull up the carpeting just to see because

to look inside an opened mouth is close enough

(with that much said it's time to move south)

the windshield reflects

yes air

but the temperature is just now

responding and still

the hand's message never sent because

even if we paint the walls the walls remain

what the body offers the room
(2)

one day you leave because you want to

                    it happens that : even breathing
requires a receipt
you give the underneath
               of your tongue

        you make it obvious   no distinctions   between
                               water and sky
you call the proper authorities   this morning   the scene
      folded   and placed
                  on the floor   the hour relinquished
the beating of wings
upstairs   still heard close enough

(in the third story a room of birds)

                    the door opened   she heard them
even before
already

knowing the conversation ended
                              a small portion of ground fenced away
                    behind it flowers
                                   bending on the page
                    the background a pressed sky

the birds

nest near
the corners   the clicking
        it catches on the stairs   she anticipates what
yesterday she forgot

        there was dripping framed was wood her skin was
                                                something
she wanted to touch

a floor in her at once the angled gesture of stomach of lung
and limb it is the limit placed like that the mouth does it air
the palm's print the taking for the throat was what was held
she held she let the body do what it had to and what it did
meant water in the throat the opening of the body's meaning
its discreet necessities of *let me hear what is outside this skin*
but not too close not to touch

you see she has all five and five

no this isn't it

look

she has symmetry on her face

and

too late this caught body

a throated leaf detaches

is this what it means to end

now is the time to take as many shells that fit in our hands

and she said *my good window* and meant (elbow bend lightly)

(bend to not break)

toward season

on the second day of spring
                    she understands
        the object the branch let loose

the thing fallen as to be replaced with throat and

her tongue used finally
not as gesture   not as evening hummed but

                a thing of its nature already
                        the sky a better recipient

on the narrow sidewalk she examines the dirt how the
stemmed knobs push into air how distribution grows from
seed into outline and curve to color laid flat later the rain
finding a home beneath the day makes its noise the coupling
of light and watermarked glass and then outside a ground
left covered let germinate awkwardly

the object given is the object let go

        she views the budding its curve and
disappearance back into branch

               the sky centers
    on one pale tone : she thinks :

if dusk
     is nailed to the wall : if breath acts
as afterthought maybe then
               the eye catches more
      between glass and reflection

underneath the gesture the bulbs left illuminating the
                  pockets of leaves
        pushed aside   the days take time

she sees reflected in the glass a face of lines one where eyes
are something still of the body that can be taken : can be
owned as in : a hand held out some petal to touch she knows
each day has variables : a phone call this morning some
type of interlude of *this was your decision* remember day :
followed by a relinquished click : but : the bricks are settled
each block placed priced and 10 people will do the same job
for less : she has the feeling what needs to be done involves
nailing : getting a signature there : right when a pause right
then : she can point prove there must be

though never easy to say this she meant

needed the coloring :
escaping from cheeks not branches but

light from the ground rises thin :
                              travels away don't forget
sunset off a boarded canary

              yesterday she knew the answers : knew the time

it takes to travel between

each day longer and the sun never sets still
the same piece   still eating whatever is given she

              understands logic : that once
she is gone she is

the setting occupied by the sudden shift of body to branch

a relationship with awkward bud she knows
nature isn't natural and she takes part
she asks questions

    of stem and leaf : what the urgency is to leave seed behind
                    why the ground's requirements persist
proof that outside
remains
even after the shutting is done

but still
          she sees how it works

the completed bloom into conversation   the branch
                             extended slight green

the pushing of color
from underneath and yet

is this what bloom is : the taking of water to color

leaf : there are the leavings to think of

the variation of tone held tight to branch

(definition borders the sidewalk
color obscures the object it covers is part of and yet)

through the last leaves dried
left still piled
on the ground
is there something to the door banging against its frame
the screen taped to keep in place or :

do you find it difficult
that you remain on one branch out of necessity
the phrasing of your form
losing its outline

you see a view becomes obstructed from chair to windowsill
glass and screen then random branches leaning up from the
ground past to pockets of new growth green against brown to
sidewalk and more mixings against the siding of a house up
to windows the carving of sculpted white paint chipping then
to more lines and lines meeting up to the arrowed point of
the roof raising itself to the same washed color of sky

(and then

and then admitting somehow an object in its environment
watches   a taken to leaf on branch   the slowness from
ground to sky

doesn't matter the names or the counting or the framed
scene from outside it looks like day   the location lost
though the stairs locate to door and handle though the view
admits of water)

                    it's before the actual budding
takes place a certainty of given days

the object will appear and usually with color   an extension
of stem and fiber

but not yet but waiting won't but it will be one morning one
look out the window one sudden shift of view and there it
will be as though it always was

about the washington prize

biography of water is the winner of the 2004 Word Works Washington Prize. Carrie Bennett's manuscript was selected from 339 manuscripts submitted by American poets.

FIRST READERS:
> Nancy Allinson
> Dean Blehert
> Doris Brody
> Christopher & Charlene Conlon
> Deanna D'Errico
> Michael Gushue
> Erich Hintze
> James Hopkins
> Tod Ibrahim
> Sydney March
> Mike McDermott
> Steven B. Rogers
> Angelin Tubman
> Jill Tunick

SECOND READERS:
> Karren L. Alenier
> Bernadette Geyer
> Jonathan Vaile

FINAL JUDGES:
> J.H. Beall
> Cynthia Hoffman
> Miles David Moore
> Ann Rayburn
> Hilary Tham

about the author

CARRIE BENNETT is a graduate
of the Iowa Writers' Workshop
where she was a recipient of
the Maytag Fellowship. She
earned her BA and MA from
Florida State University. Her
poetry has appeared in *So to
Speak, 88, Phoebe,* and *The
Bellingham Review.*

Photo by Lilly Roberts

about the artist

KELVY BIRD was born in the Hudson River Valley and holds a
BFA in Painting and a BA in Art History from Cornell Uni-
versity. Her paintings, exhibited in the greater Boston area,
aim to generate inquiry into our understanding of relation-
ship. She serves as co-coordinator of Vernon Street Studios
and volunteers for activities that increase the presence of
art in the public sphere. Kelvy also works as a process and
graphic facilitator in the field of organizational development.

For more information, please visit: **www.kelvybird.com**

about the word works

The Word Works, a nonprofit literary organization, publishes contemporary poetry in collectors' editions. Since 1981, the organization has sponsored the Washington Prize, a $1,500 award to an American poet. Monthly, The Word Works presents free literary programs in the Chevy Chase Café Muse series, and each summer, free poetry programs are held at the historic Joaquin Miller Cabin in Washington, DC's Rock Creek Park. Annually, two high school students debut in the Miller Cabin Series as winners of the Young Poets Competition.

Since 1974, Word Works programs have included: "In the Shadow of the Capitol," a symposium and archival project on the African-American intellectual community in segregated Washington, DC; the Gunston Arts Center Poetry Series (Ai, Carolyn Forché, Stanley Kunitz, and others); the Poet-Editor panel discussions at the Bethesda Writer's Center (John Hollander, Maurice English, Anthony Hecht, Josephine Jacobsen, and others); Poet's Jam, a multi-arts program series featuring poetry in performance; a poetry workshop at the Center for Creative Non-Violence (CCNV) shelter; and the Arts Retreat in Tuscany. Master Class workshops, an ongoing program, have featured Agha Shahid Ali, Thomas Lux, and Marilyn Nelson.

In 2005, Word Works will have published 57 titles, including work from such authors as Deirdra Baldwin, J.H. Beall, Christopher Bursk, John Pauker, Edward Weismiller, and Mac Wellman. Currently, The Word Works publishes books and occasional anthologies under three imprints: the Washington Prize, the Capital Collection, and International Editions.

Past grants have been awarded by the National Endowment for the Arts, National Endowment for the Humanities, DC Commission on the Arts & Humanities, Witter Bynner Foundation, Writer's Center, Bell Atlantic, Batir Foundation, and others, including many generous private patrons.

The Word Works has established an archive of artistic and administrative materials in the Washington Writing Archive housed in the George Washington University Gelman Library.

Please enclose a self-addressed, stamped envelope with all inquiries.

The Word Works   PO Box 42164   Washington, DC 20015
editor@wordworksdc.com   www.wordworksdc.com

word works books

Karren L. Alenier, *Wandering on the Outside*
Karren L. Alenier, Hilary Tham, Miles David Moore, eds.,
  Winners: A Retrospective of the Washington Prize
* Nathalie F. Anderson, *Following Fred Astaire*
* Michael Atkinson, *One Hundred Children Waiting for a Train*
Mel Belin, *Flesh That Was Chrysalis* (CAPITAL COLLECTION)
* Peter Blair, *Last Heat*
Doris Brody, *Judging the Distance* (CAPITAL COLLECTION)
Grace Cavalieri, *Pinecrest Rest Haven* (CAPITAL COLLECTION)
Christopher Conlon, *Gilbert and Garbo in Love*
  (CAPITAL COLLECTION)
Moshe Dor, Barbara Goldberg, Giora Leshem, eds.,
  The Stones Remember
* Linda Lee Harper, *Toward Desire*
James Hopkins, *Eight Pale Women* (CAPITAL COLLECTION)
* Ann Rae Jonas, *A Diamond Is Hard But Not Tough*
Myong-Hee Kim, *Crow's Eye View: The Infamy of Lee Sang,
  Korean Poet* (INTERNATIONAL EDITIONS)
Vladimir Levchev, *Black Book of the Endangered Species*
  (INTERNATIONAL EDITIONS)
* Fred Marchant, *Tipping Point*
Judith McCombs, *The Habit of Fire* (CAPITAL COLLECTION)
* Ron Mohring, *Survivable World*
Miles David Moore, *The Bears of Paris* (CAPITAL COLLECTION)
Miles David Moore, *Rollercoaster* (CAPITAL COLLECTION)
Jacklyn Potter, Dwaine Rieves, Gary Stein, eds.
  Cabin Fever: Poets at Joaquin Miller's Cabin
* Jay Rogoff, *The Cutoff*
Robert Sargent, *Aspects of a Southern Story*
Robert Sargent, *A Woman From Memphis*
* Enid Shomer, *Stalking the Florida Panther*
Maria Terrone, *The Bodies We Were Loaned* (CAPITAL COLLECTION)
Hilary Tham, *Bad Names for Women* (CAPITAL COLLECTION)
Hilary Tham, *Counting* (CAPITAL COLLECTION)
Jonathan Vaile, *Blue Cowboy* (CAPITAL COLLECTION)
* Miles Waggener, *Phoenix Suites*
* Charlotte Gould Warren, *Gandhi's Lap*
* George Young, *Spinoza's Mouse*

* Washington Prize winners

about *biography of water*

There's a mood, perhaps known best seated on a balcony, when the mind turns transparent as darkness falls. It's in this absence, for her an opening, that Carrie Bennett speaks. She hears a silence that grounds us, the diction of water and glass, one English among thousands. To turn the leaf in leaving, to close this door. Where do her sidewalks lead? Hush, you'll miss her answer. Not quiet words but the quieting.
–R.M. Berry, author of *Dictionary of Modern Anguish*

Reading Carrie Bennett's biography of water is like passing almost imperceptibly into a world defined by a sixth sense, a world we all knew existed as children, and that we've been patiently, hopefully holding out for as adults. Everything seen here is seen as though for the first time. Everything said is uttered against a backdrop of silence. A cosmogony of the body and of the sentence. Integrity of vision. Command of language. If this is what you feel a book of poems can and ought to do, then you have not waited in vain. It would be inaccurate to say that this is work of much promise. biography of water is a promise fulfilled.

–James Kimbrell, author of *Three Poets of Modern Korea: Yi Sang, Hahm Dong-Seon, and Choi Young-mi*